A POETRY COLLECTION

AFFECTIONS

not sleeping

•

ALSO BY

CHET DIXON

BEYOND THE TRAILHEAD

A POETRY COLLECTION

AFFECTIONS

not sleeping

•

CHET DIXON

TWEED

OGHMA CREATIVE MEDIA

www.oghmacreative.com

ISBN: 978-1-63373-241-4

Interior Design by Casey W. Cowan
Editing by Diana Ross
Cover Photo by Aimee Dixon Plumlee
Interior Photos by Aimee Dixon Plumlee and Abigail Derrick

Tweed Press
Oghma Creative Media
Bentonville, Arkansas
www.oghmacreative.com

ACKNOWLEDGMENTS

•

I WANT TO THANK DIANA ROSS, my editor, for keeping me from making many errors. I want to thank my daughter, Aimee, for making suggestions, asking good questions and typing each poem. If it were possible, I would thank every individual in person who enriched my life with their presence and nurture. They kept me alive and moving forward, and have impacted my writing immensely. Many individuals have influenced my life and work with their love, companionship and encouragement to experience this great and wonderful world which offers us freedom to live, grow, and express our feelings, passions, visions, hopes, and dreams. Thank you!

AUTHOR'S NOTE

•

WHEN I BEGAN WRITING POETRY in the 1950's, I shared what I was doing with no one. Even my closest family members were unaware that I wanted to become a writer. In high school and college, my writing had great personal importance. Like a good friend, it was there when tough times came around. It gave me healthy expression and balance.

Now, in 2017, I want to share what I write with a larger audience. *Affections Not Sleeping* is the second collection to be published of several in a series. It describes fond memories that inspire and stir the soul deeply because affections are addictive, like food for the soul.

The poems of this book shed light upon the depth of affections which have long lives and serve to identify us. They nudge us to think deeply about the lives we live in relationship to others.

FOREWORD

•

AS CHET DIXON GREW UP, he spent most of his free time along the beautiful and pristine White River of Missouri and in the deep woods of the Ozarks. It instilled a deep desire to capture both it's beauty and music for the soul. His desire to write about its romance and adventure led him to write his first poem in 1950 when he was only 12 years old. Hundreds of poems later, his first collection of poems, Beyond the Trailhead, was published in 2016. That collection clearly revealed a deep love and understanding of the great outdoors.

When Chet was a young boy there were special places that he found inspiring. He would visit them often, in secret. One special place required that he slip out of the house at night and walk through dark woods to his favorite bluff lookout high above the White River and listen to the rumbling water as it flowed over rocky shoals. Those times at the lookout, he would explain later in his life, inspired him to become a writer. These experiences gave him an open door to imagination and expression never before known to him. It created a great desire to share with others the beauty and tranquility of the Ozarks backcountry.

From his early years and on through his professional career, his poetry writing increased over time capturing different parts of his life. Now, in 2017, this new book, *Affections Not Sleeping,* shows the impact that relationships have upon all of our lives. It looks at the inner feelings we hold dear that never fade. It also shows a personal love of God and His great creations, as well as, family and friends.

This is a book that will make you think about your own past and lead you to remember how life loved, and affections not sleeping, are an important part of who each of us are.

Both of Chet Dixon's poetry collections begin to develop a snapshot of who he is. I know this because he is my dad.

Aimee Dixon Plumlee

CONTENTS

•

AFFECTIONS NOT SLEEPING

Dedicated to all my loved ones who I hold dear in my heart.

Thank you for inspiring me to become who I am and will be.

the

POEMS

•

Love stories and affections
Live on and on and
Are like cool drinks of water
Nurturing parched, thirsty souls.
We bask in their delight
And keep them safe
As they play music inside our
Imagined and remembered worlds.

SEARCHING FOR YOU

•

I saw you many times
This morning;
When the lady came by
With her boy and a girl,
Each time I was greeted
With a smile,
When I saw a lady reading
With great pleasure,
And whenever I remembered
How much I love you.

Yes, I saw you many times
This morning
And I keep looking
Everywhere.

FILLING SPACE

•

I've found a way to not
Think about you.

Work late,
Go out to eat,
Take a walk in the park,
Look at a few books,
Watch tv,
Make some coffee,
Do an hour's work,
Take a hot bath,
Go to bed—

Sleep—

Until,
Well,
Until later
If it ever begins.

REMEMBERING

•

Why do I keep silent when
Good things fill my mind.
Why do I not tell stories
Of men and women who were so kind
And who by words and deeds
Kept me from falling low,
By their unchanging character led
And taught me where to go.
They were not big and showy
Rather, small and without much sound.
They made and make life better now
Through their human kindness I found.
Now words will never reach their ears
Of accolades about life they made
But remembering as I do just now
Their memories will never, never fade.

ARDY

•

Give me space to watch your eyes
And hear your soft voice sleep

Let me steal a late night touch
As night grows ever deep.

And when we join in slumber's way
To cuddle close to await the day.

Our dreams will find our secret place
And never go away.

TAKE ME ALONG

•

Take me along when you leave,
Then with the folding eve
I can sit upon your vision.

Take me away in a secret dream,
Then when in gloom you sing
I can appear in the mist.

Take me along when the ocean roars,
Then with its rambling upon the shores
I can run to you.

Take me along when nature chimes,
Then upon the evening's wooded clime,
Stop and I will meet you there.

Take me along when you search the sky,
For there among the wild birds cry
I've sent a word and a kiss.

Take me along on every pathway,
Then forever you can hear me say,

I love you.

I love you.

STREAM

•

Trickling stream
As cotton spun
It and I merged
As one

Made me feel
Twixt and tween
Love real
And love
A dream....

Love real
And love—
A dream

SCHOOL DAYS

•

Secret feeling, almost divine
Brings an ominous youth to mind.

Morning honeysuckle, the waking quail,
The springing fields that never fail,

Tell of secrets that held my feet
Through good and bad of youth's retreat.

In silence they rest, but not alone,
Never forsaking the friends all gone.

Whether uneven or a model of man
They rest with patience the best they can.

2 1 0 5

•

Quiet and soft
Were lingering thoughts
When to my presence
Heaven brought

Kindness around
In secret words
Like cool south breezes
Softly heard....

....and almost felt.
I quietly touched
The hem of mysteries....
Sleeping.

BEFORE MORNING

•

Touch me now with
Kind words while high
Just before the morning
Wastes away to defy
My hope.

Speak to me with words
Soft and kind
And let all the world
Circle round my mind
And stop.

Take my moving hand
And help
This racing heartbeat
And seek my best
Sacred gift.

The morning will wait
And the fear restrain
And the breath of souls
Will find no pain
In secrets—
Then I'll go.

LAKE VIEW

•

Is where youth and joy
Have vanished,
Where voices and motions
Are locked in private prisons.

Strange words,
Spoken harmlessly,
Float across crowds
Wanting to give moments.

Some bodies sit and stare,
Others walk in silence
Others are stilled
Waiting for the end.

Nothing is flawless and
Grace is now a lost art.
They often shun visitors
Afraid of a critic's eye

Thoughts are hidden
Except in glassy eyes
And faint smiles.

Making friends is never easy.
They hide inside secrets.
But I am a friend.
My ears attend carefully.

You touch a hand, an arm,
And some will smile
And come in hope.
Others scurry with fear like foxes.

They search your stay
And wait for the asking
Of the least possible favor.

Nothing lasts very long here,
Except the endless wait
For waving shrouds and roses
That will come soon.

Lakeview becomes a memory
Locked in time,
Though both have now gone away.,
And now free.

SLEEPING WITH ANGELS

●

She was sleeping so bravely
With the angels
That she talked through the night

My closeness had no meaning,
The angels had no fear,
I remained silent.

But she was so humanly graceful
To her heavenly guests
That I soon dared do something less--
Than angels do.

WALK WITH ME

•

I hold you in my heart today and
Know you're close along my way.

As I travel looking straight ahead
Hold me close when tempests come and
Let my soul be fed.

The promise that you're always near is
All I'll ever need fulfilled
Your abundant truth and wisdom is
All I need instilled.

Peak my reverent attention
And reveal your truth,
Help me keep with confidence
The great enlightenment you gave
In my youth.

HERCULES GLADE

•

He cools me
With the gentle winds
He cleanses me
With the showering rain
He heals my soul
When I behold Him
And I seek Him, here.

His magic silence
Takes away all pain
His friendly voice
Sings to my soul
When I come here
At dusk or dawn
His glory I behold.

My steps are never loud
I keep them very soft
In reverence to its silence
My voice is seldom heard
For when this place
Begins to speak
It speaks without a word.
It is a sacred place.

FROM MY TREE

•

I lifted an arrow from my quiver,
Making sure it was ready to deliver.
I waited long for my prey to appear
He's on his way and soon will be here.

Without a move and very still
I knew my need I would surely fill
Then as he cautiously stepped into view
I made a choice about what to do.

As my arrow left the bow
I knew precisely where it would go.
I also knew why it was sent
As well as my honorable intent.

Then I saw blood streaming down
The side of the buck my arrow found.
I felt regret and wished for a chance
To reconsider my hunting stance.

While I always held that I harvest for food,
Deep inside I felt a change of mood.
I have no need to hunt for meat
Just to be with nature is a big enough treat.

What is happening to me eludes me for sure.
But one thing I know, this question will endure.
Will I send my arrow again?
I don't know—it depends.

1 0 1

•

Unwanted voices invaded my ear
About unfilled wishes the best I hear
Its shameless nature must pass and burn
I beg the voices to go and not return
Yet free from my power and wistful duress
The voices still linger I meekly confess
And even tuned out of the muddle I hear
It should be far away, but it lingers near.

UNTOLD FOREVER

●

I hid a wooden plane high
Tied to an oak tree limb.
It was firmly held and hidden.

It would never have been found
But soon a rainstorm
Crossed the land, and the plane
Came floating to the ground.

It revealed its secret scripts
That none would ever know,
Not even her.
It was my secret.

A man walking his fence line
Found the plane
My secret was lost,
My heart was faint,
My soul lay bare.

Laughter rose loudly
And the whole world knew my secret.
It tore me.
And even though
All talk went away
As if none remembered,
For me it would
Forever stay…. burning!

SECRETS

•

Go with me now
To the cottonwood groves,
Where the spring,
Quietly trickles away,
And evening breezes
Romance through locks of grey.

Go with me now
As the sun goes down.
We can dance and play
As shadows creep.
And when stars come out from hiding,
Secrets can be told again.

ARDY

•

You spoke so often
In songs divine
That only human
Spirits find.

Though moments then
Are forever gone,
That gentle touch
So lovely shown,

Will dwell inside…

Forever.

ECHOES IN THE MIND

•

Will you laugh again
When you return to our rendezvous,
Where we played without fear
Along sandy flowing streams,
Quiet secret forests,
Open sunny fields,
Below sycamores and willows
Where shimmering campfires
Cast ghostly shadows
And evenings slipped away unnoticed?

Will you laugh or cry
When we remember
Choosing weak and strong drinks
As we listened to chirping frogs,
In eerie streams and bogs
By dark sleepy waters?

Will you laugh or cry when we talk
In soft voices and eager whispers?
Or will you claim forgetfulness
And discard past tastes of heaven
Like bad morning coffee?

Will you laugh or cry when memories are
Enkindled and music, unwritten,
From hidden places,
Replay our songs and dances?

Will memories remain frozen in time
Never to breathe again?
Will you remember memories made?
After a while will you wish for more?
Will my tears reveal a conclusion
That the greatest affections often wither,
Giving way for time predators to steal
Pieces of heaven quietly resting
Among echoes living in the mind?

ROMANCE WITH A PHANTOM

•

I saw a phantom
Quietly gay
Waiting by a bus stop
One early Spring day.

She sang for a while
A merry melody
Then like a phantom
Disappeared from me.

As I remembered my phantom
That so quietly had gone
I grappled with a dream
That was solely my own

But wakefulness removed
What so gayly had grown
And again like my awareness
My phantom had gone.

Days slowly passed
As I hopelessly searched
Giving no promise
But a heart immersed,
In the wine of my fantasy
That so breathlessly appeared
And in quiet battle
To my heart was endeared.

The seasons passed
With no sight of my guest.
And as the seasons passed
My phantom seemed to rest.

But in the tent of my silence
I often find
The memory of my lost phantom
Still living in my mind.

And to the quiet death
Of my persistent friend,
My soul will cherish
The memory within.

Then came a day
Like a quiet melody
My romance with a phantom
Was forever lost to me.

BEAUTY AND JOY

•

Dogwoods and showers
Go hand in glove
Like early spring mornings
And two turtle doves

Both are friendly
Like two in love
Dogwoods and showers
And two turtle doves

They both embrace morning
With beauty and joy
They come all frisky
Not bashful or coy.

Oh how I envy
The joy and love
That I see so openly
In dogwoods, showers, and

Two turtle doves.

MY DEAREST

•

Take me along
When you walk
The road where you pray,
Sing,
And times when
You are silent.

Take me on pathways
That only you can walk
When your load seems heavy,
When your soul is weary
And you don't want to talk.

Listen for sweet sounds,
Familiar footsteps,
And voices often heard
But lost.
I will be nearby.

Now I'm walking
Along the same road
Holding your footprints.
I hear the same voices.
I long for you.

Take me along
As you journey on.
Let me stay to the end.
I'll remain quiet
And not make a sound.
Just take me along.

RUBENSTEIN'S SONG

●

Sing from the untouched side
The single human song,
That only I can sing or know
That only I must feel,
Alone.

Let its still sounds ever pass
Upon some waiting pad,
To find forever passage free
To make a listening soul,
Glad.

HELPING

•

When you see me stumble
Just lend a helping hand
And when I try to tell my story
Dig deep to understand.

And if in eager trying
Your help I push away
Don't stop your loving kindness
Never send it away.

PETROHUÉ

●

To this place,
Bring your troubles,
Bad thoughts,
Anger and fear,
And then lose them
After knowing
The majesty
Of Petrohué.

ALONG CUZCO STREETS

•

Little children
With soiled hands
Outreached
Begging for pesos.

They follow me
Like eager flies
Hoping a wasted particle
Will be dropped.

They seek me
As though I smell
Unlike their world
And friends they know.

Not until I give
My rich scat,
Do they scurry away.
I then rejoin my peace
And comfort…

Oh my God!
What have I done?

STRAIT OF MAGELLAN

•

Sounds of human voices
Playing lost and still,
Store away memories
In deaf mutes,
That cling to the seas,
The skies and land.

Man and beast hover
Beneath the skies
Beaten by whimsical winds.
They watch the ages pass
And visitors
Fleeing to the sun.

Above the howling winds
Of December's warm breath,
Dreams are made
With open eyes,
For soon I will
Fold my temporal tent
And let the ages pass peacefully.

And surely God
Shall rest His hand
Upon the rocks and seas
To protect
Their mystery and dread
Until another strolls close
within its grasp.

HOOKER

•

She smiled at me
When I sat alone
In the hotel lobby.

I really wanted to believe
It was meant for more
Than just that moment.

Later I saw her on the street
And wondered why
She looked but turned,

And smiled softly
To the man following.

I saved the rest of my feelings.

SILHOUETTES

●

Low lights of evening
In silhouettes gave
One life a new treasure
To relish and save,
To light the path
When no one is near
To hold a heart gently
In sadness or fear.
Now nothing will be
Worth having or holding,
For nothing compares
To this new life unfolding.
In my low light evenings
Space will be filled,
With silence and open space
Where joy has stilled.
Yet nothing ever lived
Will completely fade away.
My mind will uncover it
To live another day,
If not today or tomorrow.
But when my low lights show
Silhouettes so kind and beautiful
That I savor and know
And that satisfies my soul.

DANCE

•

Two people
Holding hands
Made me think
And understand,
The love that binds
Two souls in one
Begins new life
But never done.
And on it grows
Not by chance
But by a beautiful
Loving dance.

FIRESIDE FEELING

●

If I could only speak
The words my heart desires
I could tell you stories
Old but fresh with life.

It would give you images
Coated with memory's moss
And would hold at bay
The best fox chase.

You could hear the bugle
In the hand of a master
And the last long bawl
Of the walker's sweet tune.

And somewhere, not heard
The victorious Red Fox
Would turn and smile
Knowing everything is well.

And through the early light
Streaming across Venus
Like the shedding of night gowns
You would find a self-history.

If I could only speak
Or spread thoughts on canvas
Or set my images to words,
You would sit with me now

With inside tears falling
And longings clawing
At the heart of feelings
Wanting to live it again.

RAINDROPS

•

Nothing quiets my soul more
Than raindrops on a tin roof.
Each sound fills my mind
With memories lingering aloof.

The child returns from aging bones
When raindrops open closed doors
Closed by hurry and wait
And essential human chores.

Raindrops make my eyes close
And my body calm,
And just for a short time
I find a heavenly psalm.

YOU, FOREVER

•

You are the blossoms lifting arms
To reach my touch.

You are the breeze
Rustling through trees above my tent.

You are the evening's moonlight
Streaming across quiet meadows.

When I call to you
Your answer is hidden in echoes.

When my eyes close in slumber
You watch and guard me quietly.

When I wake your smile is waiting
With kisses.

You go on many paths with me
Willingly, without fear or hesitation.

When I leave to return no more
You will be with me . . .

forever.

OLD FRIEND

•

Our lives will change with time
Especially how we do little things.
But in the mind of old friends
How good life was still rings.

Nothing can make a dark place glow
Like having him stop by,
If only to lend a helping hand
Or just to say a simple hi.

But, now old friend of many years
This one last time I say,
I would not give away one thing
Our friendship brought our way.

I can't go on your journey home
But one thing I'll always do
Every time I'm in the woods
I'll take time to think of you.

Don't you worry
About those you left behind
We all will work to keep them safe
Along the path they find.

Clear streams and the forest green
Will be their lasting view
And as they walk their destined path
Their hearts will be with you.

So now, goodbye old friend,
I know your way is blessed.
For in God's gentle hands
Your soul will ever rest.

HISTORY FADING

●

Along a disappearing road
Each step whispers
Of men and women
And walking children
Who walked here
When signs were clearly
Printed into dirt and stone.

As each track and rut print
Slowly passes
The stories that once lived
Now pass with no voice.

This fading history
Lies vulnerable
Its stories ride
Like phantoms at dusk
With voices rising
From the entombed
To enshrine memories left
To be recorded
By an art form
Unable to capture
Its essence.

A story not lost is that
Behind a grey mare's saddle
Children rode
Others walked playfully,
Listening and singing
To the rhythm
Of uneven hoofbeats
On dirt and stone.

The horsewoman
Skillfully guided the grey mare south.
Only when evening silhouettes
Brought lowland chills
And feelings about unknown creatures
Did all voices become quiet.

Now the horsewoman,
The children,
The mare,
The signs,
Have gone away or fading.
This part of history is dying,
And will die with me forever
Unless I be the teacher.

These memories of my youth
Remain like ghosts.
They often keep me awake. . .
They haunt me.

TRAILS

•

Old trails are becoming strange now
Without even one tombstone left
To help us remember
The wagons and horses,
And running children on trails
Of stone and mud and leaves.

Now footprints hardly mark the ground
That tell history's path.
But now the voices of my youth,
Only remain like ghosts
To haunt me.

FRIEND

•

There was a reason you came along
Just in time to lend a hand
Not knowing my need you came along
God knew you would understand,
How I had a need,
How troubles abound,
How problems unsolved
Were pressing and hovering around.

You came along just in time,
Not too early, not too late.
God placed you there for a specific task
On a specific date.
Just as God made the stars
The moon and sunshine
He gave me you, a friend,
Who came along just in time.

LONGING

●

When the sun dips to the ocean floor
And stars begin to light the bay
I begin to dream of lovers playing
Along the shores in early May.

My heart keeps yearning, searching
For that city filled with glee
Where lovers find their paradise
And there I wish to be.

Please come to join my ship in anchor
Then sail with me the wider sea
We will find new worlds waiting
With love for you and me.

MISSING YOU

•

More than ever before, I missed you
In the meetings today,
When going downtown,
Walking under the Arch,
Watching the boats go down the Mississippi,
Listening to laughter, and
Watching children romp and play.
Today I really miss you.

More than I can ever explain to you,
I miss your hand,
Your words when moody,
Your smile when intended,
Your hand on my knee,
Or just a simple request
To go to the market.
Today I missed you.

I really missed you today
When I walked alone,
When a visitor sat on my bench.
My thoughts were stilled
Only for a while.
Then I remembered how much
I miss you, my love.

ALONE IN ST. LOUIS

•

Alone in St. Louis
Where the city moves
With star-like mystery,

Sounds and smells,
And latent temptations
Give way to evening pleasures.

Here above the squalid
But more than just a pauper's nest
Is found a special life.

The lights of the Robert E. Lee,
The Admiral, the tiny dotted eyes
Of an Arch holds evening at bay.

The tinge of liquid upon
Dry tongues and tired spirits
Calms troubled minds.

Some conversations grow with evening
Others murmur meaninglessly,
Some find quietness alone.

As evening welcomes night
Tables empty slowly as patrons
Disappear into the waiting morning.

Lights of the city slowly disappear
While some people of the evening
Beg for more of its spirits.

Chic young ladies are led away
To other more secret places
Not discussed.

And the night not yet ended will
Give spirit to other monuments
In this high city.

THE WHEEL

•

Some people feel so lucky
When they turn a casino wheel,

To me it doesn't make a memory
And never a special deal.

I know when I'm a lucky man
When quiet joy I feel,

Watching the deer, in my pasture
Searching for an early morning meal.

NEVER TOO LATE

•

It's never too late
To dream.

It's never too late
To have hope.

You never do wrong
Unless you give up,
Or do nothing.

AFFECTIONS
not sleeping

•

I

We met in early Spring
When days were warm and gentle
And stars sparkled at night
Like glitter holding secrets.

Often I penned your heart
Upon my pad
To wistfully commemorate
Hope and plans born
Before they washed upon rocks
Of circumstances and innocence.

11

Now when I watch the evening lights
Your eyes stare at me
And even through my aging lens
I see you look at me.

When cool evening breezes
Visit me waiting,
I touch your face,
As it slowly falls away.

You come and go
Like a phantom of the night.
You haunt me.

I I I

Every time I sit in a shade
By quiet reflecting water
With breezes playing
In hanging oak tree boughs,
I hear you call to me.
Each time I listen intently,
Motionless
Hoping to see you.

As ages pass
These places and sounds
Haunt me.
I can't escape them.

I V

The ink in my pen
Often grows dry.
Even when the well is full
It lays stoic
Without a voice
Like wasted driftwood.

Often I embrace a memory
Kissed by belief,
Driven by hope that
Fate will favor my desired fortune.

Even when the sun descends
And night comes near
I wait for you.

V

Decades have passed
Since our teens captured
Our minds, muscles and pride.
Now we grow older
Together, yet apart.

You coast in and out of my mind.
I remain imprisoned,
Looking,
Listening,
Hoping.
I hear no sound of you.
I see no image.

I search for you,
Everywhere.

V I

Deep into the night
I sit at my lookout
Waiting for the stars
And moon to show me the way
To where you sleep and dream.

Sometimes in my sleep
I hear you laugh
At my foolish dilemma.
It injures me but
I refuse to banish the mirage.
I keep running
To find you waiting for me.
It vanishes.

V I I

Sometimes in my dreams
Your eyes reflect the rising moon,
Your smile sits still,
Your presence lingers.

All through the night
I reach for you.
My reach falls short.
I keep failing.
I feel pain.

I reach into my heart
Where you stay.
You burn in me
Like a coal of melted iron.
My soul weeps for you.

VIII

I hold in my hand a flower
Pressed flat.
You would remember
Where we found it blooming
On a trail with no name.

The flower reminds me
Of our plans.
I keep holding it
To keep it safe.
I cherish it,
Wondering
Has passing time
Kept you safe?

I X

At night
I sit in my dark room.
I hear your steps,
See you walking
Along the water
On our secret trail.
You are alone.

You float around me
In mid-air, smiling
With your piercing eyes
Like birds of paradise.

Alone at night,
Thoughts of you
Haunt me.

X

My search is endless
And every door seems locked.
The keys are lost.
Only memories remain
And become ravaging floods
Tearing flesh from bones
And piercing my soul.

I will not turn loose.

I can't.

X I

Your journey has taken you
Beyond what I know.
Everything dead-ends now.
Memory is my treasure
I keep fanning my hope
And simmer in my defeat.

Tomorrow will come
And I will find you.
You will walk to me,
Touch my hand,
And you will give to me
Your everlasting smile.

Yes, tomorrow
I will kiss the wind
That you breathe
And you again,
When I find you.

MEMORIAL

•

The dark granite wall lay stoic in fluid blue.
Shadows spread upon wooden rails.
Walkers milled with quiet endless stares,
Giving and taking gifts and cares.

Captured in its reflection they say few words
Trying to connect pieces of past and present.
Not knowing how, they give honor humbly.
With heavy hearts, they gaze numbly.

With hushed voices some stood in salute
Among givers, receivers and scorners.
But all hearts stood or sat touching
Fluid blue names, with tearful mourners.

THE CROWD

•

Trailless words and laughter rise
Crowd nests swarm and
My words grow still and numb.

The evening deepened
Spirits made lewd gestures as
Words became nothing, grotesque.

Unnoticed I slip away
Beneath evening lights and stars
To find a gentler sound.

Far from the crowd
The evening I once sought
Still lingered within me.

Soon, the troubles lifted
My soul found its rightful place,
Unshackled.

WASTING AWAY

•

This chatter sounds like hell
Visited by ten thousand
Jesters and elated women.

It feels meaningless, like the
Sound of wild geese
Running aimlessly.

My mind becomes jelly
Reacting to shock—
Shivering inside.

I waste away—

I am alone—

I wish you were here!

FRIENDS

●

Let the forest grow
Tall and dense
Even if to many
It makes no sense.
Let the acorns fall
To cover the ground.
Make each seed rich
And each one found.

Then as my friends
Find evening treasure,
That nature supplied
With heavenly pleasure,
I'll hide in secret
But not to harm
To watch God's world
And majestic charm.

Then without a sound
I'll slowly slip away
Filled with wonder
And wanting to stay.
But they and I

Have places to go
Our destinies different
Among friends and foe.

But for a short while
Our spirits rest
As they fed on acorns
And I, their secret guest.

MY DREAMS MY JOURNEY

•

I can sit and wait
At the starting gate
Or get up and begin
To conquer my fate.

I can keep on hoping
That my dreams will appear,
Or begin my journey
And conquer my fear.

I can begin very soon
To get my win
Stop looking back
Wanting to begin.

As I get older though
I keep thinking about dreams
Yet knowing so well
I'm running out of steam

When I'm really being honest
I know it's getting late

I keep getting older
And I haven't left the gate.

I know I'm getting older
And my dreams are beginning to fade

Though weak and frail
I must accept the bed I've made.

I'll never completely lose
Those dreams of long ago
I know I must begin my journey
That only I can know

My dreams, my journey
All belongs to me
I'll just hobble on my way
Where I should already be.

LIGHT

•

Light sends away the dreaded dark
To cure every hurt and snare
Light is sent with special power
With all God's love and care.

Light heals the abandoned broken hearts
And reveals the robber's lair
When danger threatens to block our way
God's light is always there.

Light wets our ravaged, dusty world
And gives the rain to make things grow
We need not fear the darkest times
Just stand without fear and know…

God's light is always there.

WILDERNESS

•

The wilderness never obeys me
Nor tells me how to act.
It offers its unique nature
And always holds nothing back.

God is like the wilderness
Hovering all around.
In the wild, you feel His presence
As you listen to every sound.

In the wilderness, you hear His spirit teaching,
You bask in His perfectness.
In the wilderness God is easily found,
A place He chose to bless.

In all its natural wildness
When its stillness and harshness unfold,
They who trod a wilderness place
Its' splendor they'll always hold.

PRAISE

●

I am a minute speck of dust and
You, my Lord, all love and grace,
Why do you watch over me?
Why have you always cared, and
Even more, shared
A love that set me free?

Who am I, my Lord, among the stars
That you should love and want
To take my cares away?
And if I never understand,
One thing I know for sure.
Inside your loving care I'll stay.

I am so small in your universe,
An unknown fragile matter
That took a breathing life.
Even small, without worth,
You hold and keep me safe
As I walk through worldly strife.

As a servant of yours, my Lord
I shall never stop to rest
Without an act of praise.
As your servant I'll stand in awe
Of your marvelous heavens and earth
And my hands to you I raise.

SHINING PEBBLES IN A PASSING STREAM

•

They shine when quiet waters pass
To wherever they choose to go.
They shine when torrents rage landscapes
Disguising their even glow.
Then when waters clear again
They return as from a dream,
And lie so quietly as before
As shining pebbles in a passing stream.

SONG

•

My soul awakens
When church bells ring
At the beginning
Of each new day
Their lovely melody
Touches my heart
Their messages
Come to stay
To me they speak
A song of praise
To the greatest joy
And peace God gives
They tell me
That all is well
And that today
I can begin to live
I praise your wondrous
Name my lord
You lift me up
In every way
Lord give my feet
A higher plane
A place for me
To safely stay
You are the only
Thing I need
Down here

Or up with You
Tell me Lord
Guide me Lord
To whatever
You have me do
Tell me Lord
Guide me Lord
In whatever
You have me do.

PART OF LIFE

•

Life is
feeling a cool breeze after a summer day
viewing a thousand vistas from my feet to the distant horizon
hearing chirping birds in fields and along my bluff
observing children playing in the heat of competitions
seeing soaring eagles and vultures floating in updrafts
watching the red and grey foxes eagerly searching for a meal
feeding friendly deer and turkey then watching them and
falling to sleep as raindrops play music on a tin roof
This is part of life

Life is
feeling the pain of a deceased, long–lasting friendship
seeing a wildfire ravage a stand of virgin pine and fir
feeling helpless as snow and ice melt and seas rise
hearing a baby's cry when its mother cannot return
feeling the earth violently shake beneath your feet and anxiously
anticipating aftershocks
hunting for a lost plane somewhere on land or beneath the sea
listening for a call for help but unable to bridge the gulf to rescue and
watching war dismantle and destroy the lives of young men and women
This is part of life

Life is
accepting risk as normal but growing to fear it
being a strong caregiver to being cared for as a child
knowing where light is shining but unable to walk out of the dark

moving from proactive, to reactive, to inactive, unwillingly
realizing the necessity of lifelong choices then finding it easy to ignore them
giving up control and power to a growing desire for safety and security
being praised for excellence then relegated to something old, outdated and
obsolete and living with purpose
being persistent and patient to becoming unsure, weak and dependent
This is part of life

Life is
having courage and hope and facing sunshine or storms
when you know the deck is stacked against you- you never stop
putting hope in the place of despair and defeat
giving help without knowing the who or why or how
teaching what you know to others so they can grow beyond you
writing and talking about honorable values and virtues and
walking unclear trails to provide safe passages
waiting for the sunrise to cure the aches of dark times
fighting the fear of losing while struggling to hear the victor's song
praying with no doubts that your prayer is heard and
submitting to the call of your heart and honoring your time and space on earth.
This is part of life

Life is
joy, comfort and beauty
it is pain, fear and disorder
it is created new then grows old and
it has a spirit born of courage and hope that
can transform the torn and worn body and ravaged soul to live
and forever journey forward

All this is part of life

WESTBOUND ON 66

•

Travelers keep going, never stopping
Vision fixed upon their goal.
Lodges waiting for their guests
Hoping luck will fill their roll.

Eyes of travelers strained from gazing
Needing beds and dinners hot
Moving onward following dreams
Tired, worn, but not ready to stop.

Sunlight dropping, stars appearing
Travelers begin a search for sights
Of something special on 66,
The magic of flashing neon lights.

Then begins their anxious talking
And getting closer they begin to laugh
Knowing soon their legs can walk
To stretch their tired, aching calves.

Eager to see the city limits
Its' magical, glowing, moving lights
Travelers now in strange surroundings
Search for restful dreamy nights.

Later on, an alarm clock sounds
They hurriedly take breakfast waiting
It's time to go and hit the road
It's getting late and daylight's wasting

Away they go on down the highway
Where cars and trucks are all a mix
Going somewhere in a hurry
On the endless Route 66.

HIS LIGHT

•

His light sends away dark times
So they cannot hurt us more
He sent us light to show a path
That we could not see before.
The light will lead us on
To a safe and heavenly place.
Then at the end when time is gone
Our souls will abide within His grace.

FEEDING TIME

•

A turn at the spoon
Endeared a quiet chuckle
While feeding my baby
His blueberry buckle.

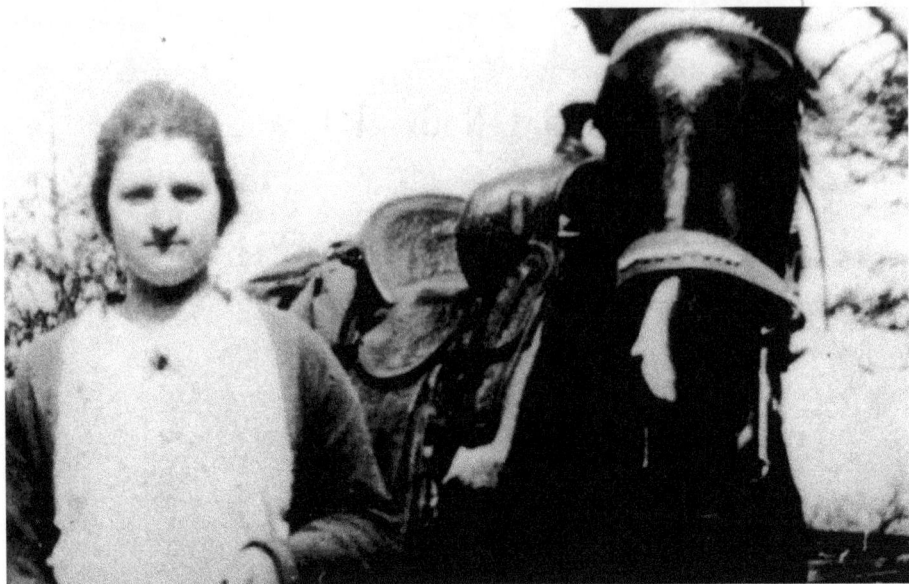

THE HORSEWOMAN

•

The horsewoman
Skillfully guided the grey mare south
Through eerie dense forests,
Across swift streams,
Hoping to beat the sunset
And starless dark.
Not until evening shadows
Brought lowland chills
And fears of rumored creatures
Did playful voices become still.

On the road
Small children rode safely
Behind the grey mare's saddle.
Others walked playfully
Listening and singing

To the rhythm
Of uneven hoofbeats
On dirt and stone.

The old, narrow road,
Now a hunter's trail,
Lost in a forest
Is slowly disappearing
And almost home again.
Whispers in the mind
Rekindle its spirit and grace
Where men, women and eager children
Walked to far away places.
Only faint signs remain
Etched in solid earth.

As each track and rut print
Slowly passes by,
Stories of wagons, horses and families
Pass with no voice.

Memories and history lie,
Vulnerable and entombed,
Waiting for someone to
Capture their essence.

Now the horsewoman,
The children,
The mare,
The signs
Have gone away or fading.
These memories of youth
Remain with me like ghosts,
They sometimes haunt me,
And will die with me forever
Unless I be the teacher.

CREATION ARTISAN

•

The sound of patting feet,
The lick of an anxious tongue,
And the sudden squeal
Of a voice young,
Hurries the mother's chore
Of custard and corn
Until a little artisan
Is someday born

A PRAYER

•

If you choose me Lord to do a job
That's ok with me.
I know it's a duty I cannot shirk
Your servant I choose to be.

Your endless love so graciously given
May choose me to go or lead,
In places so small yet profoundly great
To lift one soul in need.

Your gifts so wrapped in arms of grace
Waits for me to speak,
A word that only I can speak;
A word that I must keep....
Yes, Lord.

CHET DIXON GREW UP IN the Ozarks backcountry. He was born in a log cabin built by his father and went to a one-room schoolhouse that had 12-18 students each year. He considers growing up in the country a rich background for his life of work and writing.

After growing up in the Ozarks, his desire to explore the world led to several universities and a diverse work history. In his early twenties, he worked with migrant workers in the fruit harvests of Oregon and Washington and served as a fishing guide on Missouri lakes and rivers. He later worked for city and state governments in leadership positions. He was also a consultant to the Missouri Women's Council of the Missouri Department of Economic Development. His work experience includes speaker, trainer, workshop leader, writer, strategic planner and consultant for personal and organizational change. He is a businessman and President of Ministries of Love, Inc., an organization that builds Christian schools in Chile, South America.

His publications include *Learning, Changing, Leading: Keys to Success in the 21st Century,* co-authored by Sue McDaniel. Chet and Sue McDaniel also co-authored fifteen basic training documents used for consulting work with the Missouri Women's Council. His first collection of poetry, *Beyond the Trailhead,* was published in 2016 by Tweed Press.

Chet has the strong belief that we must never stop learning, changing, and leading as we each help create a great 21st century.

www.chetdixonpoet.com   •   www.blog.chetdixonpoet.com

www.ingramcontent.com/pod-product-compliance
Lightning Source LLC
Chambersburg PA
CBHW031629040426
42452CB00007B/737